D1358141

THE PRACTICAL STRATEGIES SERIES
IN GIFTED EDUCATION

series editors
FRANCES A. KARNES & KRISTEN R. STEPHENS

Fostering Creativity in Gifted Students

Bonnie Cramond

WAGGONER LIBRARY
DISCARD

WAGGONER LIBRARY
TREVECCA NAZARENE UN

PRUFROCK PRESS, INC.

Copyright ©2005 by Frances A. Karnes
and Kristen R. Stephens-Kozak

All rights reserved.

No part of this book may be reproduced, translated, stored in a retrieval system, or transmitted, in any form or by any means, electronic, mechanical, photocopying, microfilming, recording, or otherwise, without written permission from the publisher.

Printed in the United States of America.
ISBN-13: 978-1-59363-173-4
ISBN-10: 1-59363-173-1

At the time of this book's publication, all facts and figures cited are the most current available. All telephone numbers, addresses, and Web site URLs are accurate and active. All publications, organizations, Web sites, and other resources exist as described in the book, and all have been verified. The authors and Prufrock Press, Inc., make no warranty or guarantee concerning the information and materials given out by organizations or content found at Web sites, and we are not responsible for any changes that occur after this book's publication. If you find an error, please contact Prufrock Press, Inc. We strongly recommend to parents, teachers, and other adults that you monitor children's use of the Internet.

Prufrock Press, Inc.
P.O. Box 8813
Waco, Texas 76714-8813
(800) 998-2208
Fax (800) 240-0333
http://www.prufrock.com

Contents

The Practical Strategies Series in Gifted Education offers teachers, counselors, administrators, parents, and other interested parties up-to-date instructional techniques and information on a variety of issues pertinent to the field of gifted education. Each guide addresses a focused topic and is written by scholars with authority on the issue. Several guides have been published. Among the titles are:

- *Acceleration Strategies for Teaching Gifted Learners*
- *Curriculum Compacting: An Easy Start to Differentiating for High-Potential Students*
- *Enrichment Opportunities for Gifted Learners*
- *Independent Study for Gifted Learners*
- *Motivating Gifted Students*
- *Questioning Strategies for Teaching the Gifted*
- *Social & Emotional Teaching Strategies*
- *Using Media & Technology With Gifted Learners*

For a current listing of available guides within the series, please contact Prufrock Press at (800) 998-2208 or visit http://www.prufrock.com.

Introduction and Assumptions

Is it possible to teach someone to be creative? Is it possible to teach someone to be intelligent?

In both cases, I'd say the answer is "no." But, we can teach students to use the creativity and intelligence they have. We can teach them to think more creatively and/or intelligently. We can encourage them to value, practice, and evaluate their own creativity or intelligence. And, we can teach them strategies for thinking more rationally or imaginatively.

Do all people need to be taught creative strategies? No, of course some people intuitively develop their own strategies for breaking through creative blocks. They know how to transition from one mode of thinking to another easily. In the same way that some people learn to read without instruction, or others seem to come wired with natural mathematical ability, there are individuals for whom creative ideation is natural.

Then there are those who need some instruction to learn to read, some teaching on how to solve math problems, and some help with logic and creative strategies. They may not use these techniques all of the time, but rather use them to develop their own shortcuts or pull them out when they are really stuck. Just as the study of logic can help most individuals learn to think more logically, so, too, can the study of creative thinking techniques train individuals in thinking creatively. Just as the dispositions related to critical thinking can be recognized and nurtured, so can the dispositions related to creative thinking be developed.

So, first let's begin with some assumptions:

1. Creativity is valued.

2. Everyone has some creativity, and it can be nurtured.

3. Creative strategies can be taught.

4. Creative dispositions can be encouraged.

The issue of creativity, according to a structure described by Rhodes (1961, 1987) as the four P's—Person, Process, Product, and Press (i.e., environment)—will also be detailed in this publication. These components of creativity, individually and in combination, help us examine its wonder by looking at its parts. But, creativity, like so many other marvels, is more than the sum of its parts. So, although the components will be explored separately, a discussion of the synergy of creativity—the interaction of the parts, and more, that result in the magic of the creative act—will follow. Because it is the primary component in terms of setting the stage for teaching creativity, the Press, or environment, will be examined first.

Teachers who wish to encourage creativity should first examine the classroom climate. Factors in a creative classroom environment include psychological safety, intrinsic motivation, opportunities to learn about and pursue their interests, and opportunities for both stimulation and quiet reflection. Challenges should match the students' abilities, and blocks to creativity should be removed. Take the self-test below to see how suitable your classroom environment currently is for creativity. Rate each item from 0–3:

0 = Seldom or never
1 = Occasionally
2 = Sometimes
3 = Usually

_____ 1. Students are safe from ridicule from their peers.

_____ 2. Activities are interesting to the students.

_____   3. Students make choices about what they learn.

_____   4. Students are involved in stimulating activities.

_____   5. The work is too hard for the students.

_____   6. Students are encouraged to learn from their failures.

_____   7. Students who come up with weird ideas are accepted.

_____   8. Students enjoy learning.

_____   9. Students make choices about how they learn.

_____   10. There are times and places for quiet reflection.

_____   11. The work is too easy for the students.

_____   12. Students are encouraged to examine the things that block their creativity.

Scores for questions 1 and 7 test the principle that the classroom is *psychologically safe* (Rogers, 1976). For these items, the higher the total score, the better. The classroom should be a place where students feel they can propose unusual ideas without criticism from their peers or teacher.

The responses to questions 2 and 8 reflect the degree of *intrinsic motivation* (Amabile, 1983) that is involved in most activities. Realistically, no classroom will engage students 100% of the time. No classroom should encourage creativity 100% of the time either. Students have to learn that there are lessons that must be learned even when they are not interested in them. They also must understand that there are times to be creative and times to think in other ways. It is not practical, for example, for students to think of a creative solution for an algebra problem on an SAT exam. At such times, it is more efficient to use the learned formula.

Responses to items 3 and 9 indicate whether students have *opportunities to learn about and pursue their interests*. Again, the higher the scores, the more likely students will have some autonomy and involvement in making decisions about their own learning. As such, they have more opportunities to express their creativity in the school setting (Torrance, 1999, 2002).

In order for students to develop their creativity, they need *opportunities for both stimulation and quiet reflection*. Constant stimulation hinders creativity as much as too little stimulation (Torrance, 1965). The ideal answer for question 4 is 1 or 2, and the ideal answer for question 10 is 2 or 3. The optimal environment is one that is balanced.

In a perfect world, the answers to questions 5 and 11 would be 0. For maximum creativity, the work should be challenging to the students, but within their grasp. If the work is too hard, it is frustrating; too easy, and it is boring. When the *learning challenges are matched to the students' abilities*, they are more likely to experience the flow of optimal experience and creativity (Csikszentmihalyi, 1990).

Finally, high scores for questions 6 and 12 indicate that students are encouraged to examine and *remove the blocks to their creativity* (Adams, 1986). Students who are encouraged to learn from their failures come to believe that failures are survivable. The ramifications of trying something different are not too harsh. They learn to take the psychological risks that are necessary to develop new ideas. Also, they are able to examine the things that develop or hinder their own creativity in order to create or choose the most optimal situations for themselves.

Once the conditions that are most conducive to creativity are understood, it is a small leap to conceptualize how the environment must be constructed to encourage creative thinking. Although there are certain restrictions about how much our environment can be configured, we can control certain aspects of it. Most teachers are able, through some creative problem solving, to arrange for a place and time for quiet reflection.

Person

Although teachers have little control over the types of students who come into their classes, teaching is all about shaping the students. So, the person part of creativity is dependent upon the teacher's ability to recognize characteristics of creative individuals and nurture them. This can be more difficult than it sounds because many of the characteristics that enable students to be creative can have negative manifestations in a classroom.

Think of one of the most difficult students you have taught and mark an X on the line between each pair of descriptors to indicate where that student would fall.

Open to Ideas .... Fails to Finish

Curious .... Nosy

Risk Taking .... Thrill Seeking

Spontaneous .... Impulsive

Strong Self-Concept .... Conceited

Persistent .... Stubborn

Courageous .... Nervy

High Energy .... Hyperactive

Reflective .... Daydreaming

Independent .... Social Isolate

Now, do the same for the most creative student you have taught. Where do they fall in relation to each other? Aren't the descriptors reflective of others' perceptions of the same basic characteristics? Or, maybe they are degrees of behaviors (Cramond, 1994a).

For example, some of the personality characteristics that are linked to creative individuals are openness, curiosity, risk taking, strong self-concept, persistence, and courage. However, these characteristics, which enabled Marie Curie to become the first female professor at the Sorbonne and win two Nobel Prizes in two different areas of science, might be seen as negative traits in a student. Openness can be seen as failure to finish things, curiosity can be nosiness, risk taking can be thrill seeking, and so on. The way that these characteristics are perceived can depend in part on one's global view of the student as creative or troublesome. How these behaviors are manifested can also depend upon the student's level of development. Because creative giftedness is developmental, a student who has the high energy necessary to be a productive creator in adulthood, for example, may seem to have too much unharnessed energy in childhood.

A case in point is Nikola Tesla, scientist and inventor. As a child, his exploits of high activity and physical risk taking got him into several dangerous situations. For example, he tried to fly off the side of a building, was chased by crows and wild hogs, almost drowned in a vat of milk, and impulsively jumped on and loudly ripped the train of a woman's dress while she was leaving church (Cheney, 1981). Yet, he used this energy to work side by side with Thomas Edison in the lab, often going without sleep while their coworkers dropped from exhaustion. His risk-taking behavior, which almost killed him in childhood, was later transformed into an adult form of risk taking: gambling. However, this characteristic was also behind his ability to try new and innovative ideas that led to many discoveries.

A more humorous example is the cartoon character Calvin from the comic strip *Calvin and Hobbes*. The premise of the comic strip is the disparity between Calvin's imaginative world where his pet tiger, Hobbes, is a living, talking companion, and the adult world based in stark reality. One comic strip has Calvin swinging at recess. In the next panel, the bell rings and Calvin continues to swing. Then, a classmate asks him if he hasn't heard the bell signaling the end of recess. Calvin responds that it takes him more than one recess to wear himself into a state of submission.

Educators should recognize children like Nikolas and Calvin as creative individuals who can learn to focus their energy productively. Torrance (1982) found in his longitudinal study of creative individuals that having a mentor was critical to children's ability to retain their creativity. Many times, these mentors were teachers who had recognized and valued the creativity of the individual in early childhood.

Teachers should also nurture the latent creativity in those who may not appear to be very creative. Some of these children, like the architect Frank Lloyd Wright, are daydreamers who grow up to be productive. Others may have their creativity nurtured just enough to learn to solve their daily life problems more creatively. Teachers cannot accurately predict which students will grow up to be eminent creators, manifesting what is called "big C," or everyday creators, manifesting "little c."

However, they can prepare all students to use whatever creativity they have more productively by creating the most optimal environment possible, recognizing and valuing creativity, and teaching students creative strategies.

Process

There are so many strategies for enabling creativity that they cannot all be demonstrated here. Following are just a few of the kinds of lessons that can be used to increase creativity.

Warm-Ups

Just as one must warm up before beginning any strenuous physical activity, so too should individuals warm up to creative thinking. Warm-ups are important in order to help students transition from the emphasis on right answers and logical thinking to creative thinking.

> We try to loosen up our thinking, to break down our concern for rules, right answers, and time limits, and to focus instead on ideation, the process of thinking up many ideas . . . playing with thoughts . . . (Treffinger, 1980, p. 33)

Humor

There are many activities that can be used as warm-ups. One is the use of humor. Depending on the age and sophistication of the students, the type of humor that is most appropriate will differ. However, most students can appreciate visual humor such as cartoons. Some teachers are on the lookout for appropriate cartoons for their classrooms all the time and keep clippings of good ones to use with relevant classes. Wonderful sources can also be found in books, on the Internet, in the newspaper, and in other print resources. Some suggestions for specific sources appear in the Resources section at the end of this publication.

Verbal humor can also help create a relaxed, positive, and creative atmosphere. Important criteria for cartoons or jokes for the classroom are:

- the students find them enjoyable;

- they are suitable for the students' stage of development;

- they are positive; and

- they are appropriate for school.

Of course, taking the humor one step further by having the students create their own cartoons, captions, or jokes is even more facilitative of creative thinking.

Brainstorming

Another technique that is useful for warm-ups is brainstorming. Most people are familiar with the process of brainstorming that encourages students to generate ideas by deferring judgment and coming up with a large quantity of ideas. Most of the time, these activities are done orally or in writing; however, there is no reason that brainstorming, as a warm-up, could not be conducted by drawing, movement, or sound.

An example of brainstorming through drawing is to give students copies of inkblots, incomplete figures, or simple line drawings and have them add ideas to make a meaningful picture or pictures. A variation of this has students trading papers after a certain amount of time to add to someone else's drawing or even turning a partner's drawing upside down or sideways to reconceptualize the shapes before adding on (Cramond, 2004).

Brainstorming through movement might include anything from thinking of new ways to pass a basketball, to creating new dance moves, to moving as many ways as possible without leaving the area next to the desk. Brainstorming with sounds might include making as many bird sounds as possible, creating raps, or tapping different rhythms.

There are many ways that students can brainstorm, depending on the class. A tasty one in a cooking class might involve adding different things to cookie or muffin batter.

Ideation Techniques

Ideation techniques provide a structure for generating ideas. These techniques are useful at the beginning of a creative activity or whenever someone is stuck in the creative process. Although we are all familiar with the term "writer's block," writers are not the only creators who need a nudge from time to time to get the creative juices flowing. Ideation techniques can provide that nudge.

SCAMPER

SCAMPER is an easy mnemonic that students can use to help them think of many and varied ideas (Eberle, 1996). The letters in the word SCAMPER represent the cues for ideas. So, for example, if students were trying to think of many different modes of travel, they might use SCAMPER like this:

Substitute   air jets for wheels on a train to make the ride smoother

Combine   a car with a helicopter to fly above the traffic jams

Adapt   the wheels of the car so that they could turn sideways to make parallel parking easier.

Magnify   the windows of the car so that visibility to drive is improved

or Minify   the size of a train so that individuals could drive them

Put to other uses the sides of the car so that people can sell advertising space on them

Eliminate   the keel of a sailboat so that its flat bottom can sail across shallow lakes and swamps

Reverse   the steering mechanism of a bus so that it can go either way like a New Orleans streetcar

or Rearrange   the bumpers of a car so that they go all around for protection.

This mnemonic device can help students who get stuck when thinking of ideas. A group of industrial designers in Taiwan even claim they often use this method when thinking of new designs.

Analogical or Metaphorical Thinking

Both analogies and metaphors are used to compare similar things. The word *analogy* is used more often in science and mathematics, while the term *metaphor* is used more often in language. But, the style of thinking is the same.

The basic technique of metaphorical thinking is comparing two apparently unlike things. For example, if trying to think of a metaphor for friendship, the students might brainstorm several things. For example, friendship is like . . .

. . . a book. It can be hard to get into in the beginning, but if it is good, you hate to see it end.

. . . the weather. There are highs and lows, sometimes there are chills or storms, but it is glorious when it is beautiful.

. . . a chair. Best when it is comfortable and worn.

. . . a bank. You get out what you put in.

Synectics

Synectics is a dialectical method of solving problems using analogies and opposites created to help businesses such as Coca-Cola, Nestle, 3M, Universal Studios, and IBM come up with innovative solutions and new products (Gordon, 1961). The process was named from the combination of the Greek *syn* (meaning bring together) and *etics* (meaning diversity) because it requires that one force-fit responses. Although developed for business, it can be used for problem solving in other settings, as well, and with a wide range of ages.

A simple use of this technique is to choose two concepts by chance and force them to fit by indicating some of the ways in which they are alike. For example, if a list of concepts were generated and numbered from 1 to 12, one could roll dice to get the number of the first word. The second roll of the dice would give the second word. Any roll that goes off the board or lands on an edge is a 1. Then, the first participant must think of ways in which the two concepts are alike. For example, suppose the following list of 12 concepts were generated:

1. acorn	5. dog	9. harness
2. bee	6. ear	10. ink
3. corn	7. folder	11. judge
4. car	8. globe	12. kite

So, if a 2 were rolled first and a 9 were rolled second, the participant would have to think of ways that a *bee* is like a *harness*. A *bee* is like a *harness* in that they both can sting. If we think of the *bee* as a quilting bee, than it can be like a *harness* in that both are related to work. If we think of a *bee* as a spelling bee, then both provide ways in which one can show how practice and control lead to good performance.

Other ways of generating chance pairs could also be used, such as randomly picking words out of a dictionary, writing vocabulary words on index cards that are shuffled and selected, and writing words on sticky notes and putting them on the sides of a game spinner. The important thing is to force a fit between two seemingly unlike ideas.

To use synectics for problem solving, force-fits are generated and applied as realistic solutions for the problem. For example, if students are trying to solve the problem of where to store supplies in the class, they might use synectics to think of creative ideas. According to Gordon (1961), there are four mechanisms that can be used to create suitable analogies. These mechanisms force the individual to consider making the familiar strange, and frequent practice with them causes such creative thinking to become habitual.

The first mechanism, using *direct* analogies, has the students make actual comparisons with similar situations. A direct comparison with nature may lead to the question, "How are supplies stored in nature?" Squirrels store nuts in trees; other animals store things underground. So, perhaps the supplies can be stored in the walls or under the floor. This could lead to a solution that involves taking less classroom space because there are floor panels that lift for storage or wall sections that open to reveal shelves between the walls.

A *personal* comparison has the student identify with some aspect of the problem. So, the students may ask themselves how they would like to be stored if they were the materials. This may lead to the idea of sleeping in a hammock, which could lead to the idea of suspending netting from the ceiling to hold supplies.

A *symbolic* comparison has the students put two conflicting aspects of the problem together or objectify the problem in some other way. So, students might try to think of a way to combine the problem of lack of room with abundance of materials. How can we fit more in less space? Perhaps the solution would be to scan many of the materials and store them electronically, perhaps on CD-ROMs.

Finally, *fantasy* comparisons use imaginary ideas to find ideal solutions. What would be the perfect solution if one didn't have any limitations? One fantasy idea—at least a fantasy in most schools—would be to have more space for storage. So, how could we get more space? This may lead to an idea such as building a library loft in the classroom or adding a storage building outside.

Although all of the types of comparison might not be necessary to find a solution, it can be surprising and fun to examine the kinds of ideas that arise from thinking in these ways. As with brainstorming, it is important to defer judgment during the ideation phase. Emphasis should be on thinking of as many ideas as possible and hitchhiking on other people's ideas. Practice with these methods may help students learn to think more fluently and flexibly.

Lateral Thinking

de Bono (1970/1990) has developed many methods to apply what he calls "lateral thinking"—deliberate thinking tools to break away from the rut of traditional thinking. Many of these methods are symbolized by trigraphs, which stand for the main ideas of the method and reminders of how to think outside of the rut. For example, *Examine Both Sides* (EBS) emphasizes keeping an open mind and delaying closure when considering a controversial issue. *Plus, Minus, and Interesting* (PMI) is used when considering and analyzing new ideas. OPV reminds us to consider *Other People's Views,* and *Aims, Goals, and Objectives* (AGO) should be kept in mind when considering a course of action. *Consequences and Sequel* (C&S) considers the ramifications and fallout of decisions. An example of how these tools might be used follows.

Suppose the class is examining the issue of whether there should be school choice and vouchers. The students could be reminded to do research and EBS, presenting the information on both sides of the debate as objectively as possible. Then, they might do a PMI analysis, listing in three columns the ideas they think are pluses for school choice, minuses, and those that are just interesting facts. The latter might require more investigation, or they just may not be easily classified as plus or minus. This could lead to a role-play exercise in which the students take on roles as parents, students, school personnel, taxpayers, or other stakeholders in the decision. In these roles, they can try to view the situation according to *Other People's Views.* Somewhere in the study of the issue, students would analyze the *Aims, Goals, and Objectives* of school choice and the current method of assigning students to schools. A concluding activity might involve examining the *Consequences and Sequels* of switching to school choice versus the current system.

Another de Bono device is the *Six Thinking Hats* (1985). This strategy can be especially appealing to younger children, but graduate students seem to enjoy it, too. This method helps individuals discuss an issue systematically, ensuring that viewpoints are expressed without being impeded. Using this method, students get into groups of six and choose or are assigned a colored hat. Students may actually don hats they make from colored construction paper or felt, or they may simply have a colored hat-shaped card in front of them as a reminder. Some physical reminder is helpful, as well as a visible chart of what type of thinking each colored hat represents. The colors and the position the holder of that color should take are:

- *Yellow—Positive.* The person wearing this hat is charged with presenting the positive side of any idea and being very upbeat.

- *Red—Emotional.* The person who takes this perspective ensures that any emotional issues related to the discussion are brought out.

- *Blue—Organized.* The wearer of the blue hat ensures that the discussion moves along in an orderly fashion, individuals stay on task, and time constraints are met.

- *White—Neutral.* It is the task of the individual wearing the white hat to state facts, restate information as clarification, and provide information without any emotional or evaluative comments.

- *Black—Negative.* This individual takes the opposite tack of the person in the yellow hat. It is this person's job to present negative components or consequences during the discussion.

- *Green—Creative.* The person with the green hat must generate new ideas and have an open, creative attitude in all discussion.

A group discussion will be certain to explore all sides of an issue. At first, students may need frequent reminders to stay "in role." However, the discipline of taking a particular role in a discussion can actually be freeing. Students can fully express themselves without concern about peer pressure regarding their views.

Here is an example of how a discussion using the six hats method might proceed.

Blue:	We are here to talk about whether the U.S. should have entered World War II earlier.
White:	How much earlier?
Blue:	That is part of what we will talk about.
Black:	I think the whole war was such a bad experience for our country . . .
Red:	So many people died!
Yellow:	But a lot of good came from it, too: the GI Bill, which allowed many people to further their education, medical and technological advances . . .
Green:	Maybe we can talk about how we might have settled the issues without having to go to war.
Red:	Not go to war? After they launched a sneak attack?!
Black:	Yeah, that seems like it would have been a mistake.
Blue:	Let's look at the events leading up to the war and what the U.S. knew when.

White: We should look at both sides of the issue.

Red: Both sides? That's not very patriotic!

Blue: White is right. We have to look at this informa-
            tion objectively to come up with a rational
            decision.

Green: Maybe we could also try to use some creative
            problem solving to see how the different coun-
            tries could have solved their problems in a less
            violent way.

Blue: We can do that, too. I suggest we proceed this
            way. First, research and delineate the major
            issues. Then, create a timeline of events. Then,
            see what options we think the U.S. may have
            had along the way. Finally, we can try to think
            of a better solution to the problems than war.

Yellow: That sounds like a good plan.

This is an idealized discussion, of course, but it is one that could occur among individuals who are familiar with the technique. With the assigned roles, it is easier for one person to be the organizer and others who don't have the black or red hats to withhold negative or emotional comments. This can be especially effective when students are assigned a role that is not one they would naturally assume. Thus, the usually negative student might be given the yellow hat and the emotional arguer would have to wear the white hat. It is also effective when discussing less complex issues when students can take turns wearing the various hats.

Another use of this technique is to have students observe and analyze a debate or discussion and decide which roles the participants are assuming throughout. Making them aware of the roles in the discussion process helps them use the roles as necessary or avoid unproductive roles when they debate an issue.

The above was just an example of some strategies that might be combined to look at a particular issue. However, it should be noted that these strategies could be used independently or in other combinations. The Resources section at the end of this publication contains additional sources where de Bono's work can be further explored.

Products

The fourth P, *product*, is the one that many see as the ultimate goal of creativity. Yet, creative people themselves often report that it is the process, rather than the product, that motivates them to continue to create.

A concern for teachers and others is how to evaluate creative products. To address this need, O'Quinn and Besemer (1999) developed the Creative Product Analysis Matrix. The criteria by which products are judged on the matrix are (a) novelty, (b) resolution, and (c) elaboration and synthesis. To clarify each of these characteristics of creative products, there are further breakdowns under each main category. Novelty is defined as surprising, original, and germinal. A product has resolution if it is logical, useful, and valuable. Finally, something is considered to have elaboration and synthesis if it is organic, complex, understandable, well crafted, and elegant.

Another way to look at the evaluation of creative products is according to the criteria that professionals in the field use. Therefore, artworks would be evaluated according to the criteria used in the art world, creative writing would be evaluated according to the criteria used in literature, and scientific ideas would be evaluated according to criteria in that field.

A good resource for rubrics and other information relating to evaluating products is *The Ultimate Guide to Student Product Development and Evaluation* (Karnes & Stephens, 1999). This book provides guidance for integrating creative products into the curriculum, with information on everything from planning the projects to evaluating them.

The actual creation of a rubric can be a powerful activity for the teacher and the students to do cooperatively. In so doing, the important criteria for evaluating the product are brainstormed, negotiated, prioritized, and communicated. The degree to which the students are included in designing the rubric will depend upon their maturity and experience, but it is possible and important to include the students in the evaluation process in order to help them learn the internal evaluation necessary to sustain their creativity. In other words, when students learn to evaluate their own products by their own criteria, they become less dependent upon external evaluations for determining the quality of their work. This is especially important when students are developing creative products. The inaccuracy of judging creative work, especially groundbreaking creative work, is evident when we examine the literature on the lives of creative individuals and see how many of them had their work judged poorly during their lifetimes by experts in the field.

The best-known example is Vincent van Gogh. His work now commands astounding prices at art auctions, but during his lifetime he had difficulty getting showings at galleries other than his brother's and could not sell his work. The vagaries of judging creative products are also evident in the life of Wolfgang Amadeus Mozaty. During his lifetime, Antonio Salieri's work was supported more than Mozart's, but now Mozart's work eclipses Salieri's. Because the judgment of creativity changes over time and place and the vanguards in a field may have particular problems getting recognition from those who have a stake in the status quo, it is especially important to teach students to judge the quality of their own work (Cramond, 1994b). The evaluation process thus becomes a learning experience, too.

Competitive Programs

In order to synthesize the creative components of person, product, process, and press into the curriculum, educators might consider adopting one of the competitive programs that address these components. These programs promote creativity through systemized processes that encourage the development of creative products. The products are then entered into competitions with other students and judged according to high standards.

There are several well-developed programs that provide instructional materials and opportunities for students to be engaged in creative activities in a systematic way and compete with other students. The best known in this category are the Future Problem Solving Program, Odyssey of the Mind, and the Invention Convention. For information on these and other types of competitions, see the Resources section at the end of this book.

Future Problem Solving Program (FPSP)

Using Parnes' (1981) Creative Problem Solving method, the goal of the Future Problem Solving Program (FPSP) is to help students learn about world problems and apply critical and creative problem-solving strategies to try to solve them. Students can compete at the local, state, and international levels in teams or as individuals. It is also possible for schools to participate and choose not to compete.

E. Paul Torrance began this program in 1974 to raise students' awareness of the future while teaching them communication, research, problem-solving, and group-work skills (Torrance, 1974a, 1974b). Crabbe (1982) found that the program was effective for these purposes.

Participants are grouped into one of three levels—Junior (grades 4–6), Intermediate (grades 7–9), and Senior (grades 10–12)—so they can investigate problems suitable to their developmental level and compete with others of approximately the same age. When teams register with the FPSP, they receive a copy of the first practice problem in the form of a "fuzzy" and a list of possible resources for research. Participants then use the six steps of the process to investigate the problem and propose a plan of action.

For example, the "fuzzy" might be about the problem of water shortages that are predicted to become critical in the next few years. A simplified version of what the steps might be follows:

1. *Problem Finding.* After researching the issue, students try to find all of the potential problems inherent in the fuzzy situation. These might include lack of water resources, overuse of fresh water, inefficient methods for purifying water, and the effects of pollution on the water supply.

2. *Problem Stating.* Students choose the problem they think

is essential to the issue, the most important problem, or the most inclusive problem and word it for attack. This typically follows the format *In What Ways Might We (IWWMW)*, followed by the chosen problem and any delimiters. For example, in what ways might we decrease the overconsumption of fresh water without destroying life?

3. *Idea Finding.* At this point, students brainstorm possible solutions to their stated problem by drawing upon the knowledge gained from the research. It is important to note that this process is recursive, so if students find that they do not have enough ideas, they may have to go back to step one and research some more. Alternately, they may choose to broaden or narrow their chosen problem for attack. Their solutions might include rationing, incentives for lowered water use, more efficient water-use systems, separation of potable water for certain uses, better methods for preventing evaporation, having water available only at certain times of the day, or education about the issue.

4. *Idea Evaluating.* Students choose from among the generated solutions by comparing them along selected criteria they have brainstormed. For this problem, the criteria might include efficiency, effectiveness, cost effectiveness, ease of implementation, and public acceptability. The FPSP materials and coaches' workshops help with the generation of appropriate criteria.

   The selected criteria are then listed on one axis of a grid with the brainstormed solutions on the other. Here is an example of what the grid might look like:

	Efficient	Effective	Low cost	Easy	Acceptable	Total
Rationing	5	4	5	5	1	20
Incentives	4	3	3	4	5	19
Separation for uses	3	2	1	1	2	9
Preventing evapora-tion	1	5	2	2	3	13
Education about the issue	2	1	4	3	4	14

The students work together to decide how to rate each solution. In this case, there are five solutions to rate, so the solutions are rated from 1 (lowest) to 5 (highest). This requires negotiation and consensus. After the solutions are rated, they are totaled in the last column.

5. *Solution Proposing.* This step involves more than simply choosing the solution with the highest total. In the example above, the solution of rationing got the highest score, but the use of incentives is close behind. The students may decide to combine their two highest ranked choices to come up with a solution. For exam-

ple, the solution may be to institute rationing of water with fines for overuse and incentives for conservation. Students may decide that they do not really feel this is the best solution. They may not have chosen the best criteria or not brainstormed enough possibilities. In such a case, the group could choose to go back to an early step before moving forward. For example, the group may decide that the research indicates it is agricultural and industrial uses that are the biggest consumer of water. They may choose to tweak their solutions and criteria to reflect this information.

6. *Solution Selling/Implementing.* Finally, students work on a plan to implement their idea. The scope of this plan is dependent on the age of the students and the nature of the problem. In the case of community problem solving, where students take on problems in their own communities, this is the most important component because they actually implement their solution (Terry & Bonnenberger, 1995).

This problem-solving process can also be incorporated into service-learning programs in which students get involved in the community and learn good citizenship (Terry, 2000). Such projects also help the community get involved in the gifted program and promote positive public relations between the school and community.

Odyssey of the Mind (OM)

Another international competitive program that has many students involved every year is the Odyssey of the Mind. This program presents problem-solving opportunities for students from kindergarten through college. The skills that OM promotes are described in this excerpt from their Web site:

> [Students] work in teams so they learn cooperation and respect for the ideas of others. They evaluate ideas and make decisions on their own, gaining greater self-confidence and increased self-esteem along the way. They work within a budget, so they learn to manage their money. They see that there's often more than one way to solve a problem, and that sometimes the process is more important than the end result (Odyssey of the Mind, n.d., ¶ 3).

C. Samuel Micklus began this program in 1978 with 28 New Jersey schools. He and his son, Sammy, president of Creative Competitions Inc., the administering company for OM, still develop all problems for the program.

Teams of up to seven students register and choose to work on one of five problems. These problems focus on different skills in five categories: structure, mechanical/vehicle, technical, performance, and classics. As with the FPSP, there are practice problems students work on throughout the year, judges who give the students constructive feedback along the way, and competitions at different levels. With OM, these are called regional (usually within the state) and world levels.

Major differences between FPSP and OM are that OM is designed for a wider age range and incorporates a variety of problem-solving modalities. It is great for students who enjoy constructions, technical problems, and the classics—areas that are not typically addressed in the FPSP. Students who are interested in working on real-world problems and community issues tend to prefer FPSP.

A well-known construction problem derived from OM is one that has students design a container to hold an egg so that the egg can withstand a drop from a high place without breaking. The challenge is that the container must be made from a limited list of supplies. So, students have to learn about the principles of construction in order to make a container out of drinking straws, rubber bands, and tape that will protect the egg during its fall. The test is the actual drop, and the feedback is immediate.

Invention Programs

There are also programs that teach students to use their creativity and problem-solving skills to be inventors. Two such programs are Invent America and Invention Convention.

Invent America
Invent America is a K–8 program that claims to help children in the following ways:

1. raises self-esteem through personal achievements;

2. increases parent involvement;

3. assists in the application and synthesis of knowledge;

4. helps students experience the scientific method;

5. encourages creative thinking;

6. motivates students to learn;

7. integrates the curriculum;

8. develops higher order thinking skills; and

9. enhances library and research skills.

Schools, classes, home schools, and even families can enroll to obtain the instructional materials and forms to enter the competition. Many school systems hold competitions at the school, district, and state levels before sending winners to the national contest. However, each enrolled school, home school, or family may submit one entry per grade to the national contest.

With enrollment in the program, materials are provided at levels K–2, 3–5, and 6–8. A Teacher Handbook and Student Handbook are included. The Teacher Handbook contains lesson plans and information on how to set up the program in the class or whole school. The Student Handbook has step-by-step guidelines for the invention process, from problem selection to designing the invention. An inventor's log is also included to assist in recordkeeping.

Invention Convention

The purpose of the Invention Convention is to foster the development of science skills in students in grades 1–6 while giving them opportunities throughout the school year "to solve problems, think creatively, experiment, and work with data" (Houghton Mifflin Company, 2000, ¶ 1). By having students follow the same steps and patent-application process as a real inventor, their communication and research skills are also honed.

The five steps that the program has the children follow are:

1. learning about inventors;

2. finding an idea;

3. research and planning;

4. developing and testing; and

5. the participating in the Invention Convention.

The final event is competitive, and only qualifying students' projects are entered with the possibility of winning an award. Students compete at either the primary level, grades 1–3, or in the regular convention for grades 4–6.

The Invention Convention is like a science fair that each school or school system can initiate on its own. There are reference books and related resources listed on the program's Web site (http://www.eduplace.com/science/invention).

Summary and Conclusions

This guide has provided some ideas for nurturing student creativity . These ideas can be summarized as follows:

- Provide an appropriate environment to foster creativity. An optimal environment is one where students are psychologically safe, their intrinsic motivation is fostered, and there is a balance of stimulation and quiet reflection.

- Look for creativity in all students, and recognize creative behaviors that may be seen as maladaptive by other educators. Attempt to harness the hyperactivity, daydreaming, and impulsivity that students demonstrate and refocus them into the high-activity and task-centered behavior, reflection, and spontaneity so necessary for creativity.

- Teach students the creative process to motivate, stimulate, and direct their energies toward creative productivity. Teach them ideation techniques such as brainstorming and SCAMPER, metaphorical thinking methods such as synectics, and lateral thinking sparks as described by de Bono.

- Teach students the criteria for judging their creative products and those of others. Help them set their own increasingly professional criteria and aspire to meet their goals.

- Put students into contact with other students and help them gain recognition for their ideas through competitive programs such as the Future Problem Solvin Program, Odyssey of the Mind, and invention contests, as well as other competitions and activities that are more content specific. Help all students value and use their creativity, and perhaps you will nurture the next Nikola Tesla or Calvin.

Resources

Books

Adams, J. L. (1979). *Conceptual blockbusting: A guide to better ideas* (2nd ed.). New York: Norton.

Adams, J. L. (1986). *The care & feeding of ideas: A guide to encouraging creativity*. Reading, MA: Addison-Wesley.

Amabile, T. M. (1989). *Growing up creative: Nurturing a lifetime of creativity*. New York: Crown.

Baer, J. (1997). *Creative teachers, creative students*. Needham Heights, MA: Allyn and Bacon.

Brockman, J. (Ed.). (1993). *Creativity*. New York: Brockman.

Campbell, D. (1985). *Take the road to creativity and get off your dead end*. Greensboro, NC: Center for Creative Leadership.

Charlotte, S., & Ferguson, F. B. (1993). *Creativity: Conversations with 28 who excel*. Troy, MI: Momentum.

Cheney, M., & Uth, R. (1999). *Tesla: Master of lightning*. New York: Barnes & Noble Books.

Crabbe, A. B. (1986). *Creating more creative people*. Laurinburg, NC: The Future Problem Solving Program.

Crabbe, A. B., & Betts, G. T. (1988). *Creating more creative people: Book II.* Laurinburg, NC: The Future Problem Solving Program.

Cropley, A. J. (1967). *Creativity.* London: Longman.

Dacey, J. S. (1989). *Fundamentals of creative thinking.* Lexington, MA: D.C. Heath.

Dacey, J. S., & Lennon, K. H. (1998). *Understanding creativity.* San Francisco: Jossey-Bass.

Davis, G. A. (2005). *Creativity is forever.* Dubuque, IA: Kendall/ Hunt.

de Bono, E. (1985). *de Bono's thinking course.* New York: Facts on File Publications.

de Bono, E. (1990). *Lateral thinking: Creativity step by step.* New York: Harper & Row. (Original work published 1970)

de Bono, E. (1985). *Six thinking hats.* Boston: Little, Brown.

Eberle, R. F. (1996). *Scamper: Games for imagination development.* Waco, TX: Prufrock Press.

Fleming, M. L., & Hutton, D. W. (1983). *Mental imagery and learning.* Englewood Cliffs, NJ: Educational Technology.

Fryer, M. (1996). *Creative teaching and learning.* London: Athenaeum Press.

Gamez, G. (1996). *Creativity: How to catch lightning in a bottle.* Los Angeles: Peak.

Goleman, D., Kaufman, P., & Ray, M. (1992). *The creative spirit.* New York: Dutton.

Gordon, W. J. (1961). *Synectics.* New York: Harper & Row.

Gordon, W. J. (1968). *The metaphorical way of knowing.* New York: Harper & Row.

Hanks, K., & Parry, J. (1983). *Wake up your creative genius.* Los Altos, CA: Kaufmann.

Henderson, M., Presbury, J., & Torrance, E. P. (1983). *Manifesto for children.* Athens: Georgia Studies of Creative Behavior.

Karnes, F. A., & Riley, T. L. (1996). *Competitions: Maximizing your abilities.* Waco, TX: Prufrock Press.

Khatena, J. (1984). *Imagery & creative imagination.* Buffalo, NY: Bearly Limited.

Koberg, D., & Bagnall, J. (1991). *The universal traveler: A soft systems guide to creativity, problem-solving, & the process of reaching goals*. Menlo Park, CA: Crisp.

Leboeuf, M. (1980). *Imagineering*. New York: Berkley Books.

Michalko, M. (1998). *Cracking creativity: The secrets of creative genius*. Berkeley, CA: Ten Speed Press.

Osborn, A. F. (1979). *Applied imagination*. New York: Charles Scribner's Sons.

Parnes, J. S., Noller, R. B., & Biondi, A. M. (1977). *Guide to creative action*. New York: Charles Scribner's Sons.

Parnes, S. (1981). *The magic of your mind*. Buffalo, NY: Creative Education Foundation.

Parnes, S., & Harding, H. F. (Eds.). (1962). *A source book for creative thinking*. New York: Charles Scribner's Sons.

Piirto, J. (1992). *Understanding those who create*. Dayton: Ohio Psychology Press.

Piirto, J. (1999). *Talented children and adults* (2nd ed.). Upper Saddle River, NJ: Prentice Hall.

Radford, J. (1990). *Child prodigies and exceptional early achievers*. New York: The Free Press/Macmillan.

Runco, M. (Ed.). (1996). *Creativity from childhood through adulthood: The developmental issues*. San Francisco: Jossey-Bass.

Safter, H. T. (1993). *Exiting from within*. Buffalo, NY: Bearly Limited.

Springer, S. P., & Deutsch, G. (1985). *Left brain, right brain*. New York: Freeman.

Starko, A. (1995). *Creativity in the classroom*. New York: Longman.

Sternberg, R. J. (1986). *Intelligence applied: Understanding and increasing your intellectual skills*. New York: Harcourt, Brace, Jovanovich.

Torrance, E. P. (1963). *Guiding creative talent*. Englewood Cliffs, NJ: Prentice Hall.

Torrance, E. P. (1979). *The search for satori and creativity*. New York: Creative Education Foundation.

Torrance, E. P. (1999). *Making the creative leap beyond*. Buffalo, NY: Creative Education Foundation Press.

von Oech, R. (1983). *A whack on the side of the head.* New York: Warner Books.

von Oech, R. (1986). *A kick in the seat of the pants.* New York: Harper & Row.

West, T. G. (1991). *In the mind's eye: Visual thinkers, gifted people with learning difficulties, computer images, and the ironies of creativity.* Buffalo, NY: Prometheus.

Willings, D. (1980). *The creatively gifted: Recognizing and developing the creative personality.* Cambridge, England: Woodhead-Faulkner.

Winner, E. (1996). *Gifted children: Myths and realities.* New York: BasicBooks.

Zdenek, M. (1983). *The right brain experience: An intimate program to free the powers of your imagination.* New York: McGraw-Hill.

Environment Web Sites

Innovation Network
http://www.thinksmart.com

This Web site is aimed toward creating communities for innovation in businesses, but many of the ideas can be easily applied to the classroom instead of the workplace. There are helpful articles, an annotated bibliography, links for inspirational messages, self-quizzes, activities, and related links. For information on designing an ideal creative environment, go directly to http://www.thinksmart.com/2/articles/idealenvironment.html.

Humor Web Sites

Daryl Cagle's Professional Cartoonists Index
http://cagle.slate.msn.com

This site allows teachers to use the cartoons in their lessons without getting additional permission. On the *Teacher Guide* link there are lesson plans for elementary, middle school, and high school in the social sciences, art, journalism, and English.

Humor Project
http://www.humorproject.com

This site provides information on an international conference, speakers' bureau, publications, and other programs for fostering humor. There are also discussion boards, a daily article, interviews, jokes, funny stories, and *laffirmations*.

Thinking Skills Web Sites

Edward de Bono's Official Site
http://www.edwdebono.com

The official de Bono Web site contains information about de Bono, his books, courses, community projects, the creative team, and available courses.

Brainstorming.co.uk
http://www.brainstorming.co.uk

This British Web site has many links for brainstorming techniques, books, quotes, products and services, and so on. The page on Scamper is especially good.

Techniques for Creative Thinking:
Yes, They Work by Gary A. Davis, Ph.D.
http://www.winstonbrill.com/bril001/html/article_index/articles/1-50/article6_body.html

This article, available online or in print, describes several techniques for using analogical thinking to derive creative ideas.

Creativity & Innovation in Science & Technology by Mycoted
http://www.mycoted.com

This site features several creative techniques, as well as puzzles, quotes, and relevant links.

Robert Alan Black's Creativity Site
http://www.cre8ng.com/welcome.shtml

This site contains articles, activities, and other information about becoming more creative.

Competitions Web Sites

Invention Convention
http://www.eduplace.com/science/invention

This event is designed to encourage students to apply basic science.

Odyssey of the Mind
http://www.odysseyofthemind.com

This is the Web site of an international educational program that provides creative problem-solving opportunities for students from kindergarten through college.

Future Problem Solving
http://www.fpsp.org

This site features curricular and cocurricular competitive, as well as noncompetitive, activities in creative problem solving.

References

Adams, J.L. (1986). *Conceptual blockbusting: A guide to better ideas* (3rd ed.). Reading, MA: Addison-Wesley.

Amabile, T. M. (1983). *The social psychology of creativity.* New York: Springer-Verlag.

Cheney, M. (1981). *Tesla: Man out of time.* New York: Prentice Hall.

Crabbe, A. B. (1982). Creating a brighter future: An update on the Future Problem Solving Program. *Journal for the Education of the Gifted, 5,* 2–11.

Cramond, B. (1994a). Attention-Deficit Hyperactivity Disorder and creativity: What is the connection? *Journal of Creative Behavior, 28,* 193–210.

Cramond, B. (1994b). We *can* trust creativity tests. *Educational Leadership, 52*(2), 70–71.

Cramond, B. (2004). Developing creative teaching. In F. A. Karnes & S. M. Bean (Eds.), *Methods and materials for teaching the gifted* (2nd ed., pp. 313–351). Waco, TX: Prufrock Press.

Csikszentmihalyi, M. (1990). *Flow: The psychology of optimal experience.* New York: Harper.

de Bono, E. (1985). *Six thinking hats.* Boston: Little, Brown.

de Bono, E. (1990). *Lateral thinking: Creativity step by step.* New York: Harper & Row. (Original work published 1970)

Eberle, R. F. (1996). *Scamper: Games for imagination development.* Waco, TX: Prufrock Press.

Gordon, W. J. (1961). *Synectics.* New York: Harper & Row.

Houghton Mifflin Company. (2000). *The invention convention overview.* Retrieved December 13, 2004, from http://www. eduplace.com/science/invention/overview.htm

Karnes, F. A., & Stephens, K. R. (1999). *The ultimate guide to student product development and evaluation.* Waco, TX: Prufrock Press.

Odyssey of the Mind. (n.d.). *Odyssey of the Mind: Learn more!* Retrieved December 13, 2004, from http://www.odyssey ofthemind.com/learn_more.php

O'Quinn, K., & Besemer, S. P. (1999). The development, reliability, and validity of the revised Creative Product Semantic Scale. In G. J. Puccio & M. C.Murdock (Eds.), *Creativity assessment: Readings and resources* (pp. 77–92). Buffalo, NY: Creative Education Foundation.

Parnes, S.J. (1981). *The magic of your mind.* Buffalo, NY: Creative Education Foundation.

Rhodes, M. (1961). Analysis of creativity. *Phi Delta Kappan, 42,* 305–310.

Rhodes, M. (1987). An analysis of creativity. In S. G. Isaksen (Ed.), *Frontiers of creativity research: Beyond the basics* (pp. 216–222). Buffalo, NY: Bearly Limited.

Rogers, C. R. (1976). Toward a theory of creativity. In A. Rothenberg & C. R. Hausman (Eds.), *The creativity question* (pp. 296–305). Durham, NC: Duke University Press.

Terry, A. W. (2000). *A case study of community action service learning on young, gifted adolescents and their community.* Unpublished doctoral dissertation, University of Georgia, Athens.

Terry, A. W., & Bohnenberger, J. (1995). *ABLE program: ACT-I-on plan book.* Knoxville, TN: The ABLE Program.

Torrance, E. P. (1965). *Gifted children in the classroom.* New York: Macmillan.

Torrance, E. P. (1974a). Interscholastic brainstorming and creative problem solving competition for the creatively gifted. *Gifted Child Quarterly, 18,* 3–7.

Torrance, E. P. (1974b). Ways gifted children can study the future. *Gifted Child Quarterly, 18,* 65–71.

Torrance, E. P. (1982). "Sounds and images": Productions of elementary school pupils as predictors of the creative achievement of adults. *Creative Child and Adult Quarterly, 7,* 8–14.

Torrance, E. P. (1999). *Manifesto for children.* Athens, GA: Torrance Center for Creative Studies.

Torrance, E. P. (2002). *The manifesto: A guide to developing a creative career.* Westport, CT: Ablex.

Treffinger, D. J. (1980). The progress and peril of identifying creative talent among gifted and talented students. *Journal of Creative Behavior, 14,* 20–34.

Bonnie Cramond is an associate professor of gifted and creative education in the Department of Educational Psychology and Instructional Technology at the University of Georgia. She is also the director of the Torrance Center for Creativity and Talent Development and a Torrance Research Fellow. In addition, she is a member of the board of directors of the National Association for Gifted Children (NAGC) and is on the NAGC President's Education Commission. She is the editor of the *Journal of Secondary Gifted Education*, is on the editorial advisory board for the *Journal of Creative Behavior* and the *Korean Journal of Thinking and Problem Solving*, and reviews for several other journals. She has had experience teaching and parenting gifted and creative children; has published papers, chapters, and a book on giftedness and creativity; and has presented at local, national, and international conferences. Currently, she teaches graduate courses in giftedness and creativity and directs activities at the Torrance Center. Her research interests are in creativity assessment and the nurturance of creative abilities.

118345